HE MADE ME OVER

My Journey to Freedom from Sexual Sins

By Aaron S. Hawkins

All scripture quotation marked KJV are from the King James Version of the Holy Bible

All scripture quotations marked NIV are from the New International Version of the Holy Bible

ISBN 978-1-71659-085-6

Jesus Recycles He Made Me Over

Published by Aaron S. Hawkins

www. jesusrecycles.net

ABOUT THE AUTHOR:

Aaron Hawkins was born in Bridgeton, New Jersey in 1969. His biological parents divorced before he was five and he was raised by his mother and step father on a farm in Millville, New Jersey. He accepted Jesus Christ as Savior at age 12 and began acknowledging the call on his life by 14. When Aaron was a freshman in high school he began writing songs that he called "Gospel Rapp" as a way to witness to his peers. In March of his senior year, Aaron had a collection of songs copy written under the title

"Before We Were Using Elevated Speeches". Aaron considers himself one of the pioneers of Christian Rap or Gospel Hip Hop. He attended Oral Roberts University in Tulsa, Oklahoma from 1987 to 1990 and his majors were Pastoral Care and Counseling.

Aaron's goal is to complete the work and answer the call God placed on his life. Aaron wrote this book to say, "I let go of my past failings, sins and shortcomings.

I forget those things that are behind and I extend my grasp as far as I can reach ahead, and I press toward the mark for the prize of the high calling of God in Christ Jesus." Philippians 3:14

Table of Contents

Dedications

Davina my beloved wife, next to Jesus Christ you are the greatest gift God could have given me. You loved me unconditionally when I was at my lowest point, and stood by me when all others would have run away. You are the true demonstration of love personified. It is by your example that I have learned to love and your prayers that I am still in Him.
You are my world and I love you.

To my three beloved sons, Rahmeer, Aaron and Jonathan: this is a small book but I pray it has a great impact on you and many others. I am 40 years old and starting to release the potential God has planted in me since birth. Don't delay, be uncompromising men of God. You have seen my mistakes and felt the cost of my sins, learn from them and do not repeat them. Don't fight God's love, it's free just accept it and go change the world. Seek ye first the kingdom of God and His righteousness and all these things shall be added unto you. Matthew 6:33

Run to your Heavenly Father.

Thanks to all who were instrumental in my coming up and breaking free. Thank you to everyone from New Hope in Cedarville, N.J., Glory Tabernacle in Bridgeton, N.J., and V.O.D. in Vineland, N.J.

I have to give special thanks and much love to Overseer Annie L. Hall and Pastors Leslie and Sherri Hall-Holland of New Destiny Ministries in Swedesboro N.J., your prayers carried me. To my current church family and adopted parents, Pastors Lynward and Dora Hunter at Rhema Word of Life Fellowship Church in Marlton, N.J., you pulled me out of a deep pit and have shown me my place in righteousness. I love you. Elder Davita Weddington thanks for your help on this manuscript and your continual prayers.

Last but certainly not least, to my Mom who stood by me whether I was right or wrong no matter how embarrassing the situation might have been, only a real mother can do that.

I love you. Dad, thank you for your confidence in me and your encouragement. It's not over until God says it's over.

Where do I start? If I were asked what difference Christ has made in me and how do I know He could help you? I would start by saying...

I was saved at 11 years old and from that day I was never ashamed to confess Him and never denied being saved even though my lifestyle communicated a denial of Him from high school and throughout my adult life. Now I understand that with salvation comes a change.

Scripture clearly says "old things become new".

2 Corinthians 5:17 (King James Version)

Therefore if any man be in Christ, he is a new creature: old things are passed away; behold, all things are become new.

I have experienced many successes in my Christian walk, won many competitions in Bible knowledge, and wrote 12 copy written songs by age 17. I was offered a recording deal at age 18. I attended a premier Christian University, was a campus leader and was very successful at street evangelism. I mentored my peers in the faith and counseled almost daily for 2 years.

What Happened? Ye ran well, but who hindered you?

Oh Wretched Man that I Am

At age 12, I was exposed to pornography in cinema graphic form and remember seeing pornographic images in magazines as early as five and six years old.

I started experimenting with sex at 13 or 14 and had sexual intercourse by 17. From that point I would experience no control over my flesh until my mid 30's. I had small successes here and there but in between failures and shortcomings negated all my successes and left a black mark in my history that only a true and powerful experience with Christ could erase.

I was 32 years old when I realized how much my childhood and adolescence affected my present life. I found myself at 32 years old, addicted to pornography, a habit that started as early as 12 years old.

Pornography brings with it all types of sexual sins; fornication, masturbation, and adultery even while confessing Christianity. It will cause you to devalue yourself and women, corrupt your views, and defile the marriage bed. In my opinion it is the most powerful satanic influence. If you allow even the smallest foothold in your life, it will consume your mind and leave you powerless against the fight of the flesh that you will face.

It will destroy relationships and is a root cause for issues in a sexual relationship between a husband and wife.

I Was an Adulterer

These words are hard to address but I must expose sin for what it is. I have spent many years willfully jumping in and out of bed with untold numbers of women. I knew God was not pleased with my behavior. I stayed out late and lied to my wife about where I was. I had relationships with co-workers, babysitters, strangers and even my best friend's wife. I kept my actions secret for almost ten years.

I could recite the Ten Commandments verbatim by age 14. I had memorized chapters 1-4 of Proverbs, and quite a bit of Psalms that I had committed to my brain. I knew adultery was wrong. I spent many years habitually repeating the same sin, I eventually suffered the consequences of those actions.

As a young man, I observed close family members involved in adulterous relationships hidden from their unknowing spouses. I believe this developed a strong influence on my life. It made my abnormal behavior seem normal and commonplace. My environment combined with an addiction to pornography brewed a storm with devastating effects that destroyed a 12 year marriage, a 14 year relationship and two children because of a life controlled by the flesh and a life not yielded to the

Lordship of Christ. My first marriage ended when my youngest son was only 4 months old.

I was asked the following two questions by a young woman and her husband who had just began pasturing a new church. "How long will you allow sin to keep you from what God has purposed for you"? and "How long will you allow it to keep you from your destiny"? I was attending a service that was held in a library and was drawn by the Spirit to get in line for prayer. I was restored back into the kingdom that day. Did my old ways just drop off that day? No, but that day I found the power to resist and to fight. You see when you've been a slave for so long you do whatever your master commands of you without question or resistance. There was a time in my life that if a woman offered herself to me, I could not say no or resist the temptation whether I was attracted to her or not.

At a counseling session with the late Bishop Arvin J Hall Sr., he called me "weak as water." However, on that day I found new strength to say "no" and let go of unhealthy or sinful relationships. I found the strength to consecrate my body to God. Bishop Hall often said that in a fight "sometimes a good run is better than a bad stand". I've learned when to stand and fight and when to run. The fight against my flesh has consumed more than half of my life and all of my adult life. I believe if I had surrendered my life to

Christ at 14, that nothing in my life would be the way it is today.

"Submit your ways therefore to God, resist the devil and he will flee from you." James 4:7

"I have been crucified with Christ and I no longer live, but Christ lives in me. The life I live in the body, I live by faith in the Son of God, who loved me and gave himself for me. Galatians 2:20

Then he said to them all: "If anyone would come after me, he must deny himself and take up his cross daily and follow me." Luke 9:23 (New International Version)

Some might think that with my education, background, talents and gifting that I would be leading a mega-ministry by this time in my life. So what happened?

Tests and temptations came again but I needed to be reminded that I had been delivered and had a testimony to help me overcome as well as provide guidance for those on a similar path.

I knew as a teenager that the call of God was on my life. I was very active in the church and knew God wanted me to do something great for Him. When I was 13 or 14 I can remember asking myself "how am I going to reach people because I don't have a testimony?"

In our old church when we had testimony service, the old folks would stand up and talk about what God had done for them, and how he brought them through. People would clap, shout, dance, and say amen in agreement to God's powerful works.

Preachers would come in and share stories of deliverance from drug addiction, drug dealing, pimping, prostitution, and adultery. By age 16 I had heard preachers delivered from every kind of sin imaginable and most had confessed salvation as children.

I never heard anybody stand up and say when they got saved that they never looked back, stopped all they use to do and kept their flesh under subjection. I'm not saying these preachers did not do that I am saying they testified about the sin and not the delivering power of God that brought them out. Did they give God the glory? Yes they did. But they didn't speak of what it took to be free.

I grew up thinking that once you got saved you

wouldn't sin anymore. If/when you did sin you repented and God forgave you, and you just kept going. If you fell again, just repent again and keep going.

This became a vicious cycle. I have learned that delivered and deliverance are two different words.

The children of Israel testified of being delivered from the hand of Pharaoh, but they were not instantly free and in Canaan feasting on milk and honey. Their deliverance was gradual and in stages, powerful and miraculous from start to finish but not instant and not easy. I found myself saved and sinning until I was sinning more than I was living a saved and victorious life.

Steal, Kill and Destroy

When I got saved I didn't need deliverance from sexual sin because I hadn't committed any. At age five the magazine I found under the mattress planted a seed, and at age 11 the video of pornography watered the seed. The seed of salvation was planted at age 12. At 15 the sin harvest was starting to manifest from kissing to heavy petting and by 17, sex.

I knew at age 13 I was called of God to do a great work. The enemy knew it too and tried to kill me at birth. I was born premature with one lung deflated and severely jaundiced. The doctors said I would never leave the hospital.

Just before college, I learned from one of the church mothers who is a lifelong friend of my mother's how much they prayed on my behalf. She said from birth God's hand was on my life. I try to think back and remember when asked "what do you want to be when you grow up?" I never said a policeman or fireman or professional athlete. I only wanted to serve God. I knew God's call and vision for my life at 15. We must understand that satan's mission is to stop the work of God so the havoc in your life has nothing to do with you. If you have spent most of your adult life pursuing sinful pleasures and being distracted from your call like me, have never heard the voice of God or know of His plan for your life, then satan has done his job. He is an expert at his job. He is a thief, and a thief's job description is only three words. STEAL! KILL!! DESTROY!!!

KILL

Plan A. You see his primary objective is to stop the work of God. He doesn't want to drag you thru 20 years of drug addiction, 20 years of sexual perversion, or 20 years of alcoholism etc. He goes for the Kill the thing he knows will definitely stop the work of God. If you are reading this book and have survived even a minor car accident, know that it's no accident. God has a Plan for you and satan is trying to stop you from realizing and carrying out that plan. Like an assassin he takes the kill shot. Sometimes he succeeds but when he couldn't stop God's plan for me in that hospital in 1969, he went to plan B.

STEAL

I am the youngest of four siblings. There are seven years between the eldest and the youngest. I had one brother, two sisters, mom and dad in the home. We had the making of a perfect family. We had a stable environment, and lived in a nice home in a decent neighborhood but around the age of four that changed. I don't have any memories of living in the home with my dad. I only remember the horror, the fights with my mother where we were trained to fight also. I remember dad's clothes missing from their room. satan knew the effect divorce would have on four young children. He drooled when he thought about the theft he could perpetrate once the strong man was removed from the home. He managed to rob and pillage to a degree that would affect our adult lives and the lives of our children.

I was married at 21 and was young, immature and nowhere close to understanding the commitment, dedication and submission it took to sustain a marriage. My desire for family and my love for God manufactured my attempt to restore what was stolen from me as a child. It was a noble attempt but satan had a plan also, and he had been planting seeds throughout my life in preparation for plan C.

DESTROY

satan is cunning, nothing is ever by chance. He calculates, assesses and re-calculates. He understands completely the concept of a seed. He has learned from his mistakes. He has studied the seed and has perfected his work. He remembers the words of God in the Garden of Eden.

Genesis 3:15

And I will put enmity between thee and the woman, and between thy seed and her seed; it shall bruise thy head, and thou shalt bruise his heel.

On Calvary's cross when Jesus gave up the ghost, satan thought it was over and that he had won and had killed the seed.

satan knows that if you put a seed in the ground it comes to life and produces many more just like itself. When I was a young man many seeds where planted. The seeds that are watered and nourished most often are the seeds that produce the most fruit. satan understood that at age five a pornographic seed planted would germinate into a habit by age 14. He knew that pornography would cause a man not to know his true purpose in a woman's life (destroy). He knew that seeing the sin seed of promiscuity for years and years as a child would dull the effects of the Word of God and make adultery easy for a newly married young man (destroy). He knew that seeing dad's clothes missing from the drawers and closets at age four or five (the seed) would make it easier for the young man to walk away when his youngest was only 4 months old (destroy). I never had the communication with my father about marriage and the pain of divorce that too would be a part of the plan to destroy.

I visited my father on weekends, holidays and during the summer. He drove me to school from freshman year to my junior year in high school and we developed a relationship. I felt how much he always loved us and he talked about how it hurt him to leave us. I never understood the pain of not waking up with your children your seed (destroy) or felt the pain of dropping them off to a home that's not your home after weekend visitation (destroy).

The Bible states that children are like the arrows in a man's quiver.

Psalm 127:4-5 (King James Version)

4 As arrows are in the hand of a mighty man; so are children of thy youth. 5 Happy is the man that hath his quiver full of them

The arrows are put into a bow and pulled back against force and launched toward a target. An archer must practice daily to perfect his craft. The archer made his own arrows perfecting them so he could shoot them straight. satan knew I could not aim my children properly as a father because I was not with them every day. I had been beaten by the same scheme as my father (destroy).

Please understand that when talking about God versus satan they are not in the same league. God is omnipresent and omnipotent He is also omniscient meaning He is everywhere always, all powerful and all knowing. satan is incapable of ever being or doing anything simultaneously on different plains at the same time. satan's arsenal consists of his cohorts and a seed. He has perfected the use of a seed.

Testimony

If you are a Christian who is in any way like me. You probably have experienced some falls and set backs in your journey. You may have even repeated addictive cycles that keep you bound, confused and feeling unworthy to answer the call of Christ, that each of us have to answer. We must answer the call to go and make disciples of all men. Those who have been redeemed must "say so". We must not be silent; we must not cower at spreading the Good News.

How do we get past our failures and shortcomings?

In Revelations 12:10-12 it says,

10Then I heard a loud voice in heaven say: "Now have come the salvation and the power and the kingdom of our God, and the authority of his Christ. For the accuser of our brothers, who accuses them before our God day and night, has been hurled down.

11They overcame him by the blood of the Lamb and by the word of their testimony; they did not love their lives so much as to shrink from death.

The accuser of the brethren is satan and he is in the earth still using the same tricks to try to stop the people of God from doing the work of God. He has been accusing you, causing you to feel ashamed and unworthy to even name the name of Christ. I have been in this place many times and God says it's time for this vicious cycle to stop. This is the word of the Lord to me:

"My son, just like when you were a young teen you are still going thru an identity crisis. You are still looking for ways to validate yourself. You still have no clue of who you are in Me. You do not understand the height and depth of my love for you. I have purchased you with a price and you are not your own. Your validation and fulfillment comes through you knowing and obeying me. I will stop the destructive cycles in your life. I will break the bonds of inferiority and self-doubt. I will give you a new mind and a new heart. The old has passed away but you keep digging it up. You need a true understanding of my love for you. Meditate on it, study it, breathe it, and ingest it. A true knowledge of my loves, depth, height, and breadth will totally eliminate self-doubt and low self-worth, inferiority, shame, guilt and condemnation. Lay hold of it. Pursue it."

The Lion, The Bear and The Giant

There is a progression of successes that God wants to bring us through. I find that all of my failures and disappointment, shortcomings and sins are easily remembered. They are like billboards down the highway of life. They are huge reminders of what went wrong. We have to get to a place where we only see the positive.

1st. The Lion

Growing up the youngest of four I dealt with verbal abuse, all types of self-doubt and inferiority, but I was given a gift of faith. I was given the faith to believe that I could go to college and no matter who or what opposed me, I did not doubt. I knew God called me to attend Oral Roberts University and I knew it early enough to put it in my yearbook statement my junior year in high school. I applied to two schools Messiah College (my plan) and Oral Roberts University (ORU), (God's plan). I was accepted to both and Messiah offered a $5000 minority grant.

My mother was clear she didn't approve of ORU. I mean this was the year the media reported that Oral Robert's had locked himself in the Prayer Tower and announced that if he didn't receive 8 million dollars for the University, God was going to kill him. I had no doubt that I heard the voice of God at 6am when my TV alarm came on and the ORU campus flashed across the screen. I had never heard of Oral Roberts, Richard Roberts, The City of Faith or Oral Roberts University but that morning I knew I was told to go. I worked all summer and saved my money. My mother told me if I went to ORU she wouldn't help me and I believed her. I didn't know anything about registering for classes or filling out Financial Aid Forms. I bought a one way airline ticket to Tulsa, Oklahoma and on August 17, 1987 at age 17 I left for ORU. Mom had a change of heart and gave me $500 and my dad did the same. With the money I saved, I started school with $1500.

That day was the beginning of my faith walk. That day I killed the lion.

I arrived in Tulsa on a Saturday, and as my cab passed the campus on the way to my hotel I thought "wow". There were no words to describe the sense of joy and accomplishment I felt that day. The campus had futuristic architecture and mirrored glass walls. The City of Faith complex was larger than any hospital I had ever seen. I knew I was not in heaven but I was someplace very close to it. I had a day-by-day fellowship with God I heard him speak clearly and talk with me just as a friend. A silent conversation ensued Sunday morning as I walked to church in the Mabee Center about a mile from the hotel. On August 18th around 10:30 a.m., the sun was blazing hot. The sun rays reflected off the mirrored glass wall of the City of Faith and onto the asphalt and me. I spoke these words out loud "Lord if you want me to be here I'm going to need a ride" he spoke back "be specific". I said "okay I'm going to need a car". I kept walking and in less than a minute, someone pulled up alongside me and asked if I needed a ride to church. He was a middle aged white man wearing a cowboy hat. He was the exact description of what I was taught to run from as a young African American boy in a predominately white town in New Jersey. I knew God had sent this man so I got in and sat near him in the service because I was thinking about the long walk back to the hotel.

Immediately after service a woman approached me. She asked me "Do you need a car?" She began to explain that she and her husband had a car they wanted to give away and I could have it if I wanted it. I thought "this is going to be some journey if things happen as soon as I say them." The next day I registered for class got my financial aid packet and moved into my dorm room.

My faith was so strong I believed I could have anything I spoke. The young man from New Jersey had an infusion of faith and satan immediately tried to stop it.

The BEAR

When David was a young boy he killed the bear that threatened the lives of his flock. I did not have an actual live bear to face but I had a bear of a battle. I continued to struggle with sexual sin on and off through my 30's. I would have success then failure, losing battles I should have easily conquered. Jesus paid it all and He conquered sin and took captivity captive so I should have been victorious. I found that it was easier said than done. David didn't just think or hope the bear would leave him and his flock alone, but he fought and realized that it posed a threat to the life of his flock and himself.

David could have hid and let the bear eat till he was full and then leave, but he was smart enough to realize that if he did not kill it, the bear would keep returning each time with a larger appetite until one day the sheep would be gone and he would be dinner. I realize that this is what we do when we don't kill the bear of sexual sins. The habits you think are small and harmless are little cubs that feed and become grizzlies. It doesn't matter if it seems like harmless conversation in a chat room, or a flirting smile and wave with the beautiful woman at work. You must slay it immediately or it will grow. Let me share how calculating and crafty satan is. I once started innocently chatting online with a young woman from Grand Rapids, Michigan. I was living in New Jersey so I did not see any chance of an issue arising. There was never anything explicit going on we only exchanged pictures and had a few conversations over a few months. Two years later my marriage was in trouble again and I decided to take a job in Indianapolis, Indiana. My wife had decided she would move the kids out after school was over later that year. I got online and started chatting in an Indianapolis chat room. I started asking questions like what are the best restaurants, night spots and entertainment. I was using a completely different screen name than I had in the past. I started a private conversation with a young lady and when she sent me a picture it was the same young woman from two years ago. She was also using a different screen name. When I sent her my photograph she did not immediately remember me. I began to explain how I knew her and asked "why she was in an Indianapolis chat room?" she responded that she had moved there two months ago. I moved to Indianapolis and you can imagine the results.

You may ask how I could have known it would result in this. You should be asking, should a married man be chatting with strangers on the internet?

Paul said in ***Ephesians 5:3 "But among you there should not be even a hint of sexual immorality or impurity.***

Have you ever walked into a room after someone left? You did not see the person but you could tell someone was just in the room by the hint they left behind such as the smell of perfume or cologne, a hot drink left on a table or a smoldering cigarette butt.

I have spent many years leaving hints or should I say nursing cubs. When I look back at my past, every nursing cub like in the story I just told you, grew into a strong grizzly that I could not control. It devoured whatever it wanted at will. The habits we think are hidden and not seen leave hints of their existence. Habits we don't kill become strong addictions. When I was 12, I saw my first porno movie. It didn't arouse anything in me at that time, but as I continued to watch them like most kids would watch an action or horror movie, I was completely unaware that I was nursing a grizzly cub. One night when I was 15 years old and alone with a girlfriend, I got my first real kiss. I lost control and started touching and feeling everywhere she would allow until finally she said stop and immediately wanted to go home. I clearly remember her words on the telephone that night. She was laughing at me about the whole experience but she said I scared her and that she felt like a piece of meat and that I was a bear. On every date after that I was not interested in watching a movie, playing a board game or having much conversation. When I got a girl alone in my car, room or in the back of a movie theater my only goal was sex. I had a reputation of being too touchy feely. Looking back from where I am now I can clearly see what happened, but at that time I thought I was supposed to act that way.

Please understand I am not writing these experiences to boast. I am very ashamed of the life I have lived. I could write a very interesting tell all book and probably make millions but I am writing in hope that my readers will heed my warnings and learn from my mistakes and stop a devastating pattern of behavior. It is only by God's grace that I am free today. I was so far and deep in the pit of sin.

Do not let any addiction rob you of your mind, your years, your family, your health, self-worth and your self-esteem.

Most men would tend to think that pornography is not hurting anything, but I will prove to you differently.

As a boy or young man, I never saw a healthy relationship between a man and a woman. I learned to interact with women by what I saw on the screen or in a magazine. It was a very twisted and distorted lesson that I thought was proper etiquette.

When I was younger I would always try to peek through the crack in the bathroom door when my sister's friends were spending the night.

I was always touching and feeling a young lady if she sat on a couch next to me when the lights were off. I did this whether it was welcome or not, I would at least try. I remember going to a friend's birthday sleepover. I was not supposed to be there but my cousin was dating the birthday girl. When I left that party I had felt up every girl there except two the birthday girl and one of my female cousins. I was completely out of control and did not even know it. After I had sex for the first time my mind became consumed with it. When I got home from school, many times I would turn right around and ride my bike eight miles back into town to see my girlfriend. I tried every day to convince her to have sex, she never gave in but I tried for weeks on end. During my senior year in high school, I began to realize that this was crazy behavior. I had applied to ORU and I believed that the campus atmosphere was what I needed.

Before long, I quickly learned that it wasn't a change of environment that I needed. I found myself in a private meeting with the campus chaplain. I had gone to the movies with a young lady and decided I would try to make some advances by rubbing on her leg. She removed my hand and laughed it off the first two times, but the third time she got up and moved. I felt so stupid on that quiet ride back to campus. She never spoke to me again, but told one of the guys on my floor and he reported it to the spiritual life department. I could have been expelled my freshman year. I didn't realize that the cub inside of me was still being fed and growing. You would think that after such an incident I would change my behavior. I wish I could say that I did, but I did not.

The reason I'm writing this is to expose sin for the ugliness that it is. The next year I met the woman who would become my first wife. We were married and I thought my battle with the flesh was over. I cried at my wedding while standing at the altar and everyone thought it was the sight of my bride that caused that reaction. It was not. I was crying because I was tired of being a hypocrite, I was tired of being displeasing to God and thought this would make it right. I would no longer have to live in sin. I could not have been more wrong. Less than a month after my wedding I had sex with a co-worker because of a dare.

My little cub was a full-grown grizzly and over the next 14 years he grazed wherever he wanted and as often as he wanted. I had no control. I could resist temptation for short periods of time but would always return to the same sins. My first marriage ended in an embarrassing divorce. My entire church knew of my unscrupulous behavior. I had slept with two different women from my church and one was the wife of my best friend. She was also my wife's best friend.

I am struggling to write about it because I do not want to give too much detail but I want to make it abundantly clear. If you are married or single, male or female and you are struggling with sexual sin you must turn from it now. A little peek at pornography will plant a seed that will germinate and grow until it dominates your thoughts.

There were times when I would masturbate six or seven times a day while watching pornography. I have even lost jobs because I had affairs with women who were my subordinates. I did not understand nor did I want to believe that pornography had such an effect on my life and my behavior patterns until very recently. I believe God gave me what I am about to share so that I would hate it and not return to it, and I believe it will help others who need to be free of its hold.

The first thing I learned is something you probably hear every day if you are a believer. You must be transformed by the renewing of your mind.

Romans 12:2New International Version (NIV)
2 Do not conform to the pattern of this world, but be transformed by the renewing of your mind. Then you will be able to test and approve what God's will is—his good, pleasing and perfect will.
Why did I find myself enslaved to sexual sins for so long? I did not actively engage in the battle for my mind.

Yes, I knew the scriptures but I did not use them to fight when the battle got hard. I just caved in and allowed my sin filled mind to control my actions. I will try to explain it this way.

Starting from age 12 to my present age, I'm sure I have watched thousands of hours of pornography. I have participated in hundreds maybe even thousands of sexual acts, and have held untold numbers of explicit conversations. If I could put all that on a counter-balance scale with very little scripture memorization on the other side, even less prayer time, very little open and honest counseling along with zero will power to change; I don't have a direct word to porn ratio to give that would tip the scales in the proper direction.

"Garbage in garbage out" is the phrase I do remember.

I realized that I had to actively get back to learning the Word of God by allowing one or two verses a day start to cleanse my mind of the visual images and memories. I had to really start to pray and get closer to God on a more personal level. I had to spend hours praying and reading the Word of God, listening to preaching and playing worship music.

The mind is hard to reprogram after years of feeding it junk, but by the power of God it can be done. I remember times after my divorce I would get home from work around 11:00 pm and get on my computer and would sit there until sunrise chatting in adult chat rooms.

How do you erase that filth?

Psalms 119:9 says, ***"Wherewithal shall a young man cleanse his ways?"*** The answer is ***"by taking heed to the Word of God."***

Second, you will need to enlist the help of a trusted friend or pastor. This person should be someone you are sure you can be completely honest with. You will need someone who will be able to administer some tough love when it becomes necessary.

Why do I need to tell someone my struggles?

A. Revelations says ***"they overcame by the Blood of the Lamb and by the word of their testimony."***

You have got to say something, open up your mouth and declare your victory over your struggle even if it has not fully manifested.

B. The strength of sexual sin is that it is hidden.

No one can see it so we often think it's not affecting anyone but me. The paradox is that it puts you in a lonely and depressed state and you seek more and more sexual fulfillment to escape the loneliness and depression. You will keep repeating the same cycle of sin until you pull the covers back yourself and expose it.

God loves us so much that he gives us chance after chance to correct it and turn from it. If we do not heed the warning signs He will allow your very private secret sins to be exposed very publicly. Please take it from someone who knows, he loves us all too much to allow us to continue being a slave to our flesh and a slave to sin. Jesus conquered sin and the flesh for our freedom.

Stand fast in the liberty where with Christ has made you free and be not entangled again in the yoke of bondage. Galatians 5:1

The Stronghold

This stronghold of sexual sin is deep rooted in idolatry. I am not a person who believes "the devil made me do it" kind of thinking. I do not believe there is an evil spirit behind every bad deed. Most of our behaviors are just our human flesh in its fallen state ruling over our minds and doing what feels good at the time. I do believe that ***"we wrestle not against flesh and blood but against principalities and powers… against the rulers of darkness of this world." Ephesians 6:12***

I am neither a biblical scholar nor historian but because of my personal research I have drawn the following conclusions.

In Colossian 3:5 Paul wrote, *"…**but put to death whatever belongs to your earthly nature"*** and he gave a list that included ***"sexual immorality, impurity, lust, evil desires and greed which is idolatry."***

When I first looked at this scripture I said because these sins are selfish in nature, Paul would be implying that we have exalted self-gratification above God and it therefore equals idolatry. This conclusion could be correct but there is a much deeper meaning here. This particular scripture was written to the Colossian church; however sexual immorality was an issue in a lot of the early churches and continue to this day. Many pagan religions before the New Testament church worshipped their gods with sexual rituals. Some even worshipped the goddess of lust and sex. These rituals no doubt originated in the pits of hell. Demonic princes are the forces behind such practices. The practice of orgies in front of large gatherings of people in ancient times was the beginning of pornography. The participants in these ceremonies were the priestesses and any willing male or female. The onlookers would cheer and believe that their participation in these ceremonies would bless their crops, entice blessings from the gods, or even remit sins. To watch pornography and/or participate in sexual sin is equal to this same idolatry.

I would further submit that this stronghold is not easily broken because our flesh naturally seeks pleasure, and these ancient demonic spirits are the same ruling principalities and powers that control the porn industry today. The worship of the sex god still continues today every time we commit sexual sins. We willingly give ourselves to the worship of another god when there is even a hint of sexual immorality. We dance with demons when we give ourselves over to sexual sins.

We must kill the bear of sexual sin.

Sermon and Obituary (Poem by Aaron Hawkins)

Sexual Immorality born 1976 died 2010
You became my friend when I was a young boy around five or six years old.
Your introduction was subtle, the comic strip type magazine I found under the mattress.
You didn't say "hello I'm pornography" you were a funny looking cartoon I didn't understand.
We hung out every chance we could when mom wasn't around. We grew up together and as I grew you did too.
You realized you started to bore me so you left for a time.
You came back as a movie, capturing my attention and dominating my every thought.
We became closer now since mom introduced you to me.
You often said, "Our friendship is secret" don't tell anyone that we are so close. They wouldn't understand what you and I share.
Looking back at my life, the evidence of our friendship has always been there.
Our 34-year friendship has come to an end. This is your home going service
I say good bye and good riddance forever.
Leave nothing behind for me I don't need it and quite frankly don't want it.

To your resting place that pit from whence you came, take with you sexual lust and impure thinking.
Pack up pornography in every form, that seemingly innocent glare and the "wow" thought that followed. Take also that borderline conversation with sexual undertones.
The smile, the wink, the stare, the flirtation or did you call it "just being friendly."
Leave no residue my old companion I bury with you, fornication, adultery, masturbation and unclean imagination.
No longer wanted never needed but you insisted I have them anyway. So I willingly give them back to you, you know, how a "good friend" should do when they have borrowed something from you.
To close this service I say I'm glad you're gone you never were my friend anyway. You only taught me wrong.
GO back to The Pit" from whence you came never return. IN JESUS NAME.
He took captivity captive (that's you) and gave gifts unto men (that's me).
So good riddance, NEVER RETURN AGAIN. I'm Free
Therefore if the Son makes you free, you shall be free indeed.John 8:36 (KJV)

Joyfully and gladly submitted
Aaron S. Hawkins

THE GIANT

I got in involved with a team of people who where trying to find housing for 35 homeless people. I was comfortable providing supplies and praying for them and with them. I was comfortable attending meeting that talked about solving the issue. In the late afternoon the day of one of these meetings I got a telephone call. A county official called to ask my assistance in finding housing for one individual. I was honored by the call but immediately upon hanging up an old familiar friend showed up. The childhood feelings of inadequacy, inferiority, self-doubt and low self-esteem stood up and crippled me. My confidence was shaken; my thoughts were flooded with doubts and fears. The next day I was so depressed I was crippled, I could not eat all morning and afternoon.

I could not concentrate and couldn't even enjoy my favorite past time watching TV. I was faced with a personal business matter that afternoon as well and when a road block was thrown up more confidence issues piled on. I was then ready to do what I had always done when depressed and feeling down like this, turn on the porn. The only thing stopping me was the accountability software installed on the computer and my laptop. I was waiting for a call back so I decided to take a drive to the video store.

What would I choose, I picked up two borderline not rated videos and I got a stir inside that said "not worth it." I left and went back home quoting memorized scriptures all the way. Thirty minutes after I got back home my phone call came and that personal matter was settled. God had come through on my behalf and I had to wonder what would have happened if I had compromised and rented that video.

It was one small victory; I later got the big picture of a much larger battle going on.

I finally realized that the pornography and sexual sins where the symptoms of a much larger issue.

The self-esteem and feelings of inadequacy were the bleeding of a much larger wound. I thought they were the issue but I was only fighting the symptoms. Let me explain it this way.

If I had sinus congestion I would take an antihistamine, a headache I'd take an ibuprofen, had a cough, I'd take a cough suppressant etc. and this is what I had been doing. I had been treating the symptoms individually but not diagnosing the root cause.

I had finally realized and identified the root cause of my symptoms and sickness.

I had identified MY GIANT.

I had "father issues"

Let me make this clear once again this is not an excuse for my actions, every sexual sin is a conscious decision to choose lust over life and horniness over holiness. Now I am choosing life and holiness and I am here shouting the words of the boy shepherd David the son of Jesse.

"Who is this uncircumcised Philistine?"

I am here realizing my identity as my Heavenly Father's loved and cherished son.

I am writing to behead the giant that has stood in the way and mocked me for so long.

My biological father left when I was four or five years old. I don't have any good memories of living in the home with him. My mother married my stepfather when I was eight. My memories of my stepfather are bad ones.

I am sure we had some good times but I don't remember them. I remember all the yelling when he came home drunk. I remember the belittling words when I didn't take out the trash or didn't feed the pigs slop.

I remember being called a "faggot" when I cried or showed emotion. I was taught a strong work ethic from my step father. We put in a full day every day from spring planting to the fall harvest. I don't remember a "good job," "well done, thank you" or" I love you" from him.

The experience I most remember with my step father was when one day after my older brother went into the Air Force. I neglected to take out the trash so when he came home from work (by way of the town tavern) he started in on me as was customary.

He had never physically hit me without my mother's permission but this day was different. He followed me all the way out back at least 50 yards distance pushing me and yelling as I carried the trash.

I started crying and the words got worse and the cursing started. Mom stepped out on the back porch and yelled, "Aaron your brother is on the phone."

At that moment something rose up in me and I dropped the trash can turned around looked him in the eye and said, "I'm going to tell my brother and he's going to come home and kill you."

I ran as fast as I could to my mother and grabbed the phone. Sobbing loudly I explained what had been happening. My brother simply said hand him the phone. I don't know what my brother said but I know although the cursing and verbal abuse didn't stop completely it was less often and he never again called me a faggot. That was my experience with my stepfather. It was not until he was old and sickly that he ever expressed any sort of love for me.

I lived with him after my divorce and as an adult our relationship was a lot different but I still never expressed my opinion or stood up to him.

My stepfather passed and those childhood hurts came flooding back. For 11 years I listened to the abuse as a child, after my mother divorced him we had a respectful relationship, but I was over 30 years old by that time. I could not bring myself to visit the hospital accept once during the weeks before his passing.

My wife convinced me to visit one more time and he passed fifteen minutes after we left his room. My step brothers made all the arrangements for his funeral and despite my calls I never got any information from them about the service. I found out through a family friend when and where the service would be held. I was the only one of my siblings to attend the funeral.

I could not help notice that there was not one picture of us anywhere. There were pictures of our home our kitchen, our farm but none of us. There was no mention of any of us in the obituary or anywhere. My mother was married to him for over 20 years, I lived with him longer than his biological children and we were erased.

It was like we never existed and for a week or so it hurt badly. I felt like he was still yelling at me from the grave "you still don't matter."

My memories of my biological father are good ones but as an adult we have yet to establish a really close relationship. My relationship with my dad really started in high school. Every experience with my dad helped boost my confidence but they came long after a lot of damage had been done. My father drove me to school my freshman and sophomore year and during that time we talked. He shared life lessons, the Bible and how he felt about us. He took me on vacation with his family and to home Bible study every Tuesday night. He encouraged my music and took me to speaking engagements and my concerts.

He challenged me to learn the scriptures verbatim. I worked with him as an apprentice at the machine shop where he was employed. He taught me that I could fix anything. He said that if I could take it apart I could put it back together and make it work. I found it to be a very useful skill when I purchased my first car and every vehicle since. The thing that stuck with me the most from my father was these following words. I don't remember where we were or what we were discussing but I remember

"you're a Hawkins and you can have any woman you

want, if you know how to talk to her."

I think we were discussing a girlfriend I had that he did not approve of. I took those words and ran with them.

I found it to be true and was determined to make it true with me even if I had to wait years to prove, I could have any woman I wanted.

I never realized the void that was created in me by the abuse of my stepfather and the absence of my biological father. I tried to fill that void with pornography and women.

The giant of "fatherlessness" could not be killed because he had not been identified.

"Who is this uncircumcised Philistine?"

In my adult life I have been slack at working on the relationship with my dad. I guess subconsciously I have blamed him for not being there to protect me as a child.

THE GIANT MUST DIE

In order for the boy to become a man he must slay the giants in his life. The symptoms of fatherlessness are all too apparent.

Low self-esteem and self-worth,

Lack of confidence and feelings of inadequacy

Inferiority complex and no self love

My symptoms were medicated with all types of sexual behaviors. The problem is that I became addicted to my self-prescribed medications. I needed more and more to lessen the pain.

What did I need to kill the giant?

David picked up five smooth stones but it only took one to knock out Goliath. The stone that knocks out fatherlessness is LOVE, The love of our Heavenly Father. The love of the Father has always been there but we find every excuse to avoid it and ignore it. It is not until we get into trouble and the devil is pushing us around and calling us names that we turn around look him in the eye and call on our elder brother Jesus. It is then that we start to know the love of the Father.

It is not easy to receive the Love of God when we have a distorted view of love or have known no fatherly love at all. Hearing my dad say "I love you" everyday getting out of the car at school at age 13 meant everything to me. Could I accept it? Did I believe it?

At 17, sex was what I understood as love so when I needed to feel loved guess what. Dad's words didn't come to mind but the filth I had watched for years did. So how do I replace all that and receive my Heavenly Father's love.

Covertly God had been sending me messages to grab hold of His love. He used everything from a personal prophetic word that could not be denied, to the pastor handing me a book entitled "Fathered by God."

My wife has asked me scores of times when was the last time I spoke to my father. The messages I thought I was preparing for ministry where actually God ministering to me about my relationship with Him. He wanted to show me that the void in my heart I've spent years trying to fill could only be filled by Him. It is a place that can only be filled by God who walks with me through the valley of the shadow of death, who leads me beside still waters, and restores my soul. It is only God who wars on my behalf and covers me with His wings who can fill this cavern size hole. I began to learn and I am still learning my father's attributes. I have known His voice from birth and even though I was disobedient to it He still loves me and pours out His mercy and grace.

When my sins caused me and others great pain my loving Father gave me more of His sufficient grace. I began to realize that I am still alive and healthy because of His love.

His words of love have healed the hurts of the past. His acts of love have given me confidence of my future.

A FATHER'S LOVE

I have 3 sons my eldest Rahmeer is at the time of this writing 18, Aaron 16 and Jonathan 8. I can only express to you a father's love by how I feel toward my sons and how I have learned that my father feels toward me.

When I got married in 2006, my wife's son Rahmeer was 13 years old. I told her that although he was not my biological son he "is" my son. I told her I would never use the word "step" concerning him. To me the word "step" has a negative meaning and from experiences with my step father I didn't want him to feel in anyway less loved, less important or less my responsibility than my biological sons. Starting and developing a relationship with a teenage boy that I literally did not know until after I married his mother was challenging. I didn't know how to show love to someone else's child. Do I give him a hug when he leaves for school? Do I take him to the park to play ball? What do we talk about on a daily basis? What do we (Rahmeer and I) do when mom is not around?

Rahmeer is an independent child, he was an only

child. He was incredibly mature for 13 or 14. He is more athletically gifted than I ever was so playing ball with him was more for his amusement than a bonding experience. I suppose he got quite a few laughs from it. I remember Aaron telling me when he was about 10 "Dad you're the worst basketball player ever." Rahmeer was kind enough to keep it to himself. I didn't know how to be a loving step father but I knew how to not treat him differently or cause him any harm. I knew that if I couldn't speak something positive then not to speak at all. I knew he would be better off just seeing some guy in the house with mom that had no voice or identity to him, than to know someone like my step father had been to me.

As time passed and occasions arose I was able to speak to him about my concerns in his behavior, his attitude toward his mother and his outlook on life. I made sure I spoke the words "I love you" no matter how awkward it felt, even if I had to send it in a text message. I also made sure he knew my confidence in his ability, what talents I saw in him and about his potential. The day he graduated from high school I was a proud father. I was overjoyed to be able to speak over his life words of love and encouragement.

Rahmeer is my eldest son and although he came to me last on our wedding day he became my eldest son who had the birthright which entitled him to his father's blessing and the greatest portion of his father's wealth.

I love him equally and sometimes
favor him more.

Aaron is my namesake; words cannot express a father's love for his 1st born son. When he was born I watched his every expression and movement. I smelled his air when he breathed, I knew his scent. You could blindfold me in a room full of crying babies and I could find him by the sound of his voice.

I had anticipated being a father. I had no concept of what a husband really was but I knew without a doubt I could be a good dad. Aaron has been an affectionate child from the day he was born up to now at 16. He still departs by giving me a hug or pound or some form of touch. Every conversation on the phone ends with "I love you". When Aaron needs something he calls but I know he doesn't call every time he wants something. He doesn't even ask in most cases. He doesn't want to be a strain on his dad, he will get by. When Aaron started playing sports in high school I had to constantly ask him "when are your games?" I knew I had to express to him that I wanted to be there and that supporting him was important to me. I knew he would not impose by asking.

Aaron thought that I only had time for work. I knew with Aaron to make myself available and don't make him have to ask for my time, if he had to ask then it would not happen.

I named my youngest son Jonathan after the best friend of David in the Bible. Jonathan by age eight has lived up to his name.

When it comes to relationships between fathers and sons this one is the most rewarding. Dad is a superhero at this age and nothing is too much to ask for and too cute to be told "no". Jonathan is a tender and gentle child. I cannot raise my voice with Jonathan as I can with Rahmeer and Aaron. Jonathan gets a gentler approach often just a raised eyebrow and a frown is enough to change any unwelcome behavior.

If I do raise my voice and threaten to spank him it is quickly followed by a hug and words of affirmation.

Jonathan still wants to sit right up under dad when watching movies. I will never forget the expression on his face the first time he got to ride in the front seat of the car with me. He yelled"shot gun" an expression he heard his older brothers use to determine who was riding in the front seat every time we travelled. He said it even though it was just the two of us in the car that day, he said "I have been waiting a long time to say that."

The everyday interactions with my sons have given me a great insight into my relationship with my Heavenly Father. It has shown me that His love for me appears differently to me depending on what stage or phase of my life I am in. The love I havefor my boys have never been more or less. It doesn't change based on their behavior or whether they took out the trash, got straight "a"s or washed mom's car without being told to do so. I realize now that no matter what state I am in God's love for me has never changed. His love for me has remained unchanged from the beginning of time until now. I have only received His love differently based on my position in him. Let me explain.

I realized early on that Rahmeer would only know that I loved him if I told him and showed him. He was not birthed to me, so the natural love between biological fathers and sons did not exist. I was a stranger to him. He had no male figure in his life so affection between him and I at that point did not and could not exist. We had a surface relationship with "I love you" on holidays and special days with cards and gifts attached. Time progressed and he realized he could ask for more and get what he asked for if I had it, or asked to use the car if I wasn't using it.

With both of us working on building a relationship, we established a father, son and friends relationship. He knows my love for him is no different than my love for Aaron and Jonathan. He knows when I have extra we are all going to feast and party. He knows when I don't have much the little I have is his if he needs it.

We were not born into God's family but he adopted us as sons. He has bestowed on us every right, privilege and authority just as his first born and only begotten son Jesus Christ.

There are times when I have found myself in trouble and just would not open my mouth and ask for help. I realize that I am at times with God like Aaron is with me. I want to carry it on my own, handle it on my own. Dad's to busy he's got more important work to do. I'm not going to even bother Him. There are many reasons why I have been at this phase or stage. I sometimes feel undeserving because of sin or just because I haven't fellowshipped with Him. I don't feel I'm important enough for Him to change His plans or drop what He is doing to attend to what I have going on right now. In my experience I am sometimes saddened to find out that I have missed a concert or a game that I could have attended or helped with a trip that I didn't know about.

Sons of The Most High must realize that our father hastens to perform His word on our behalf.

Nothing in our lives is too small to warrant His concern. Our only obligation is to let Him know about it and watch how fast He responds. The responsibility to demonstrate the love is the role of the Father. The privilege to enjoy and walk in the love is that of the beloved son.

I am finally at age 40 standing in the place of my youngest son Jonathan in relation to my Heavenly Father. Rahmeer won't ask me for anything, Aaron will ask for five dollars but Jonathan will walk up to my wife and me and says "can I have $15." With a boyish grin and expectant eyes, how can we say "no" to that face?

I am the youngest most spoiled of my mother's four children even to this day. If I say "mom I need $40 dollars" she will pull it out of her bra and give it to me. I am here today accepting my role in the family as my Father's spoiled baby boy. I get what I ask for and I'm not ashamed to ask. He said He is taking the family some place but I'm calling "shot gun". I'm in the front seat watching His moves and anticipating His turns. I am asking "what does that do Dad?" When we settle down at night I'm in the covers next to Dad on the couch. It doesn't matter what is on television. I'm just glad to be with my Dad.

Aaron's picking on me "dad"; Rahmeer won't share the game "dad". I'm staying up late and getting up early with my Dad and nobody can beat my Dad. I'm coming for it all and asking for it all. I'm expecting my Dad to give me it all because I am his baby boy and He is Abba, My loving Daddy.
Grace and Peace

Jesus Recycles

Aaron

A Closing Prayer

I prayed a simple prayer when I got the revelation of Fatherlessness. "Love on me Dad, help me receive your love and help me love myself."

I was reminded of what my eight year old son recently said to me. "I don't care if I got to sleep on the floor dad I want to come with you." This has become my new attitude, wake me up early, and keep me up late, Dad I want to be with you. I started looking at God through the eyes of my sons. Aaron once said and believed wholeheartedly "no one can beat my dad" Now when I struggle I run to my Dad. When I am being tempted and bullied I remember "no one can beat my dad". Love on me like the Father you are.

Jesus spoke a parable that I am now getting the revelation to. He said unless you come as a little child you shall not enter the kingdom of heaven. Kingdom kids have a loving Father who sent their older brother Jesus to battle and to conquer over demons, principalities and powers. He came to overcome the rulers of darkness and to take captivity captive, to triumph through His death on the cross. No greater expression of love could God give us than to sacrifice His firstborn Son so that we could be adopted into His family.

If you have struggled with sexual sin for many years like I have or maybe your issue is still just a little cub. Pray this simple prayer with me.

Heavenly Father my Daddy,
Flood me with your love, I want and need you to fill the void that I have tried to fill myself. Show me daily the depth and the height of your love. I receive it now. I renounce and repent of my sinful, lustful ways and I cut off the head of the giant called fatherlessness.

You are my loving Dad.

Amen

My Journey from here

I have spent far too many years spinning my wheels. I have spent a lot of time and too much of my talent on wasted living, worldly affections and just plain non sense. I realize that God has not changed; His plan for my life has not changed. Day by day He speaks to me reminding me of who I am in Him. I am living everyday with the realization that I am His son. He is my Loving Father and those things that He promised me from age 13 He intends to see me lay hold to. I am dreaming and dreaming big, just like the little boy asking for the new bike for Christmas. Dad has promised and he always keeps his promises. I am remembering at age 17 the gospel raps I had copy written and then did nothing else. I still have my love for music and my goal to be a pioneer in Gospel Music. I had plans to own a radio station and a skating rink. I intended to start my own record label and produce gospel music. I use to write plays and dream of seeing them on Broadway. I dreamed about preaching the gospel and laying hands on the sick. My entire vision of my life was completely about serving God and doing whatever He told me to do.

One day God spoke to me and said "I never intended for you to have a secular occupation." If you have heard the voice of God and live by what you believe He has commanded of you I guess you can imagine how this would feel.

I realize that for almost 20 years I have been out of God's plan for my life. I remember the very point in my life when I decided to stop walking in faith, get a job, and not go back to college. I can see how my life might have been/would have been completely different. I can't say that I wouldn't have made mistakes but maybe not the same mistakes. I am not complaining of where I am in life but I am keenly aware that I have greatly missed the mark of what is God's plan for my life. I am also keenly aware of the apostle Paul's words in Romans 8:28 "And we know that all things work together for good to them that live God, to them who are called according to his purpose"(KJV)

I qualify on both counts I love God and I am called for His purpose. Every situation and circumstance has worked and will continue to work to benefit me. I realize and I hope you do too, that no matter how ugly or how painful life gets, it has worked to build me (you) and shape me (you). The situations have added and not taken away from me. No matter how it looks or how I may have felt at the time it was and is for my good.

I can now begin my journey to take back what I have allowed "the thief" to steal. He has been caught and he must now repay seven times what he has stolen. I am writing to encourage you to do as I am doing. Take back your stuff, everything; it is the "law of restoration". I am going back to the beginning and reclaiming my education, my music, my ministry.

I am taking the wealth that belongs to me with interest. I am laying hold of my confidence and self esteem. I am releasing my true potential and redeeming the time. I realize that there are many books I need to write and many songs that need to be sung. There are an untold number of lives that need to be reached with the message of the Good News that Jesus Christ died for sinners. The dreams I had as a teenager can still be attained and it is God's will for me to have everything He promised.

His will is the same for your life. Don't be defeated any longer, stand up, fight and take back what is rightfully yours. No natural father enjoys seeing his children hurt, struggle and be in pain. Any father worth his salt does anything he possibly can to rescue his child from an impending danger or pick them up when they have fallen down. Our Heavenly Father is not a man and it is His good pleasure to give us the kingdom.

Luke 12:32 (NIV) reads "Do not be afraid, little flock, for your Father has been pleased to give you the kingdom."

Did I neglect to say, do not be afraid? When I look back and realize the time that I refer to as "wasted" and I think of the place I need to get too, there is a bit of apprehension and fear. I realize I cannot make this journey and be pleasing to God when operating in fear. I am reminded of the story of Peter walking on the water in Matthew 14:25-33. Peter got started on his journey when he stepped out of the boat and began to walk on the water toward Jesus. It was not until he looked around at the wind and the waves that he began to doubt and started to sink. I realize that storms will come on my journey but God is asking me to have faith and step out on the water. This manuscript is my first big step of faith in many years. I have music to produce, plays to write and homes for boys to build. I have skating rinks to buy and radio stations to run. I have concert halls and stadiums to fill, television programs and movies to produce. I have an entire generation to reach. The storm of self doubt has already tried to stir up and cause me to look left and right but my eyes are fixed on Jesus and my ears hear Him bidding me to "Come".

He is leading me on an awesome journey and I feel the same way I did the day I left for college. I felt that nothing was impossible and that I was in the center of His will for my life. I am writing to let everyone know that God will do what He said he would do in your life. It does not matter which way you may have strayed. He is a loving Father and just as in the story of the Prodigal Son, He is waiting with open arms for you to return to Him. He wants to give you a robe to signify His glory and covering on your life and a ring to remind you of your authority in Him. No matter where you have been and what you have been through "Jesus Recycles He Makes Old Things New". I know because"He Made Me Over "and He will do the same for you.

www.ingramcontent.com/pod-product-compliance
Ingram Content Group UK Ltd.
Pitfield, Milton Keynes, MK11 3LW, UK
UKHW020138250726
13967UKWH00002B/724

9 781716 590856